THE TOTALLY NINJA RACCOON JOKE BOOK

by Kevin Coolidge

Illustrated by Jubal Lee

Leave them laughing

Kevin Coolidge

The Totally Ninja Raccoons Are:

Rascal:
He's the shortest brother and loves doughnuts. He's great with his paws and makes really cool gadgets. He's a little goofy and loves both his brothers, even when they pick on him, but maybe not right then.

Kevin:
He may be the middle brother, but he refuses to be stuck in the middle. He has the moves and the street smarts that the Totally Ninja Raccoons are going to need, even if it does sometimes get them into trouble as well as out of trouble.

Bandit:
He's the oldest brother. He's tall and lean. He's super smart and loves to read. He leads the Totally Ninja Raccoons, but he couldn't do it by himself.

Kevin: What's black and white and read all over?

Rascal: A skunk with diaper rash?

Kevin: No, guess again.

Rascal: An embarrassed zebra?

Kevin: No, silly!

Rascal: A penguin with a sunburn?

Kevin: Time's up! It's *The Totally Ninja Raccoon Joke Book*!

Rascal: I don't get it. This joke book isn't red?

Bandit: This joke book is written on white paper with black ink, and you read it all over. The word read sounds like the color red. Thus the black and white and read all over, that's the joke. Get it?

Kevin: It's not funny if you have to explain the joke.

Bandit: When two words SOUND alike, but have different meanings, it's called a homophone.

Kevin: No, you hold the phone, Bandit. Yeah, I know, you told us that in *The Secret of Nessmuk Lake*. I hope you aren't going to explain every joke in this book.

Rascal: Let's just grab a cold birch beer and some donuts, and tell some jokes. I love jokes.

Bandit: Me too! Because we are...

All: The Totally Ninja Raccoons!

Q: What do librarians use to catch fish?

A: Bookworms!

Q: What kind of train eats too much?

A: A chew chew train.

Q: How do you take a photo of a one-of-a-kind lake monster?

A: Unique up on him.

Q: How do you take a photo of a tame lake monster?

A: Tame way... unique up on him.

BREAKING NEWS:

A werewolf has apparently mated with the Loch Ness Monster....

Please share this with your friends to raise A Were Ness....

Q: Why aren't Teddy Bears ever hungry?

A: Because they are stuffed.

Q: Why was the skeleton afraid to cross the road?

A: He had no guts.

Q: Why do birds fly south for the winter?

A: Because it's too far to walk.

Q: What do you call a cow eating grass?

A: A lawn moo-er.

Q: What has a foot but no leg?

A: A ruler!

Q: What did the mother cow say to the baby cow?

A: It's pasture bedtime.

Q: Hey Rascal, which paw is best to write with?

Rascal: I mostly use my right paw.

A: Neither, it's best to write with a pen.

Q: What do you call a pair of underwear that defends itself?

A: Boxers!

Q: Why are pirates called pirates?

A: They just ARRRRRR!

Kevin: What's a pirate's favorite letter?

Rascal: Oh, I know this...it's RRRR!

Kevin: You'd think so, but it's the C!

Q: What do you call a bear with no ear?

A: B!

Rascal: Our clubhouse doesn't have a number on it.

Kevin: We should address the situation.

Rascal: It was raining cats and dogs yesterday.

Kevin: I know. I nearly stepped in a poodle.

Q: What time is it when Gypsy the Cat sits on the fence?

A: Time to get a new fence!

Q: Have you ever seen a catfish?

A: No, how does it hold the fishing rod?

Q: What do you get when you cross a dinosaur with a cat?

A: Whatever it is, I don't want to be the one who cleans its litter box.

Q: How do you make a skeleton laugh?

A: You tickle its funny bone.

Q: What do you get when you cross a zombie with a librarian?

A: Dead silence.

Q: Why did Gypsy the Cat eat the light bulb?

A: She wanted a light snack.

Q: Why can't you hear a pterodactyl going to the bathroom?

A: Because the "P" is silent.

Kevin: Hey Rascal, how do you keep a raccoon in suspense?

Rascal: I don't know, how?

Kevin: I'll tell you tomorrow.

Q: What do you get when you cross a yeti with a vampire?

A: Frostbite.

Q: What do you get when you cross a yeti with a witch?

A: A cold spell.

Q: What does a vampire take for a sore throat?

A: Coffin drops.

Q: How many vampires does it take to change a light bulb?

A: None. Vampires prefer the dark.

Q: Why do dinosaurs live longer than dragons?

A: Because they don't smoke.

Q: What do you get when you cross a fat cat with a penguin?

A: A cat whose tuxedo is too tight.

Q: What monster plays the most April Fool's jokes?

A: Prankenstein.

Knock, knock

Who's there?

Boo!

Boo who?

Don't cry. I'll tell you another joke.

Q: What do you get when you cross a ghost with a cow?

A: Vanishing cream.

Q: What do you get when you cross a dinosaur with a kangaroo?

A: A lot of big potholes in the streets.

Q: Why does King Kong have such large nostrils?

A: He has large fingers.

Q: What do you get when you cross King Kong with a werewolf?

A: A howler monkey.

Q: Why are werewolves hairy?

A: Because if they had feathers, they'd be werechickens.

Q: What did the werewolf say to the skeleton?

A: "It's been nice gnawing you."

Q: What game do you play with a smelly werewolf?

A: Hide and reek.

Q: What wears a thick coat in the winter and pants in the summer?

A: A wearwolf.

Q: What do you get when you cross a werewolf and a clock?

A: A watchdog.

Q: Why can't you sneak up on a werewolf?

A: Because he's an aware wolf.

Q: What do you call a lost werewolf?

A: A wherewolf.

Q: What do you call a metric werewolf?

A: The liter of the pack.

*For more werewolves, check out *The Totally Ninja Raccoons Meet the Weird & Wacky Werewolf.*

Q: How many witches does it take to change a light bulb?

A: Just one... and she changes it into a frog.

Q: What do you get when you cross Gypsy the Cat with a lemon?

A: Sour puss.

Q: How did the ninja beat the pig?

A: With a pork-chop.

Q: What do ninjas order at restaurants?

A: Swordfish.

Q: What's worse than finding a worm in your apple?

A: Finding half a worm.

Q: Why did the banana go to the doctor's?

A: Because he wasn't peeling very well.

Q: What's worse than a giraffe with a sore throat?

A: An elephant with a nose bleed.

Two goldfish were in a tank. One says, 'Do you know how to drive this thing?'

Q: What has two humps and is found at the South Pole?

A: A very confused camel.

Q: What has four eyes and one mouth?

A: The Mississippi River.

Kevin: Would you like your pizza cut into four slices or six?

Rascal: Just four. I couldn't possibly eat six slices.

Q: Why did the farmer chase his cow across the field?

A: So he could have a milk shake.

Q: What do you call a dinosaur with no eyes?

A: Doyouthinkhe-saurus.

Q: Why didn't the skeleton go to the party?

A: Because he had no body to go with.

Q: Why was 6 scared of 7?

A: Because 7 8 9.

Q: Why do cows have bells?

A: Because their horns don't work.

Q: What do get when you cross a soda with a marsupial?

A: Coca-Koala.

Huck: Don't fart in front of me.

Finn: Sorry, Huck, I didn't know it was your turn.

Q: Where do cows go on their day off?

A: To the moovies.

Q: What's orange and sounds like a parrot?

A: A carrot.

Q: Why are zombies never lonely?

A: They can always dig up new friends.

Q: What do vampires cross the sea in?

A: Blood vessels.

Q: How do porcupines play leapfrog?

A: Very carefully.

Q: What part of a fish weighs the most?

A: The scales.

Q: Which side of a duck has the most feathers?

A: The outside.

Rascal: Did you just pick your nose?

Kevin: No, I was born with it.

Q: What did the letter say to the stamp?

A: Stick with me and we'll go places.

Kevin: Rascal, do you want to see the world's fastest magic trick?

Rascal: Yes, go on.

Kevin: Would you like to see it again?

Kevin: What did Gypsy the Cat* say when she hijacked the plane?

Rascal: I don't know, what?

Kevin: Take me to the Canary Islands.

*Gypsy the Cat is the main adversary of The Totally Ninja Raccoons. You can read all about her in their adventures.

Q: What happened to the cat who ate a ball of wool?

A: She had mittens.

Q: What is invisible and smells like bananas?

A: Monkey farts.

Q: Why did the nose cross the road?

A: It was tired of being picked on.

Q: What's hairy, scary, and has a pair of underpants on its head?

A: An underwear wolf.

Q: What is a penguin's favorite family member?

A: His Aunt Artica.

Q: What do you get when you cross a werewolf with a forest?

A: Fur Trees.

Q: What monster is the best at hide-and-seek?

A: A where-wolf.

Q: Why did the ghost need a tissue?

A: Because he had a lot of boo-gers.

Q: What does a panda ghost eat?

A: Bam-Boo!

Q: What do you get when you cross a werewolf and a snowman?

A: Frostbite.

Q: What do monsters do with their mouthwash?

A: They gargoyle it.

Q: What do you get when you cross a werewolf with a tree?

A: A monster whose bark is worse than its bite.

Q: Where did the police put the vampire?

A: In a blood cell.

Q: Why did the turkey cross the road?

A: To prove he wasn't a chicken.

Q: Where does a werewolf keep his coat.

A: In his claw-set.

Q: What did the werewolf do after he was told a joke?

A: He howled with laughter.

Q: What is a cat's favorite dessert?

A: Mice cream.

Q: Why can't your trust the Loch Ness Monster?

A: There's something fishy about him.

Q: Why wouldn't the werewolf eat the clown?

A: He tasted funny.

Q: What type of mail do famous werewolves get?

A: Fang mail.

Q: What do you get when you cross a pig with a unicorn?

A: Pig-asus!

Q: What does a black belt eat for lunch?

A: Kung food!

Q: What do cats like to eat for breakfast?

A: Mice Krispies.

Q: What is three feet long, has a tongue, and fourteen eyes?

A: Bigfoot's sneakers.

Q: What do you get when you cross Bigfoot*
with a pumpkin?

A: Sa-squash.

*The Totally Ninja Raccoons have met Bigfoot
in their first adventure.

Q: Why don't cats play poker in the jungle?

A: Too many cheetahs.

Q: What is a cat's favorite color?

A: Purrrrple.

Q: What's smarter than a talking cat?

A: A spelling bee.

Q: What state has the most cats?

A: Pet-sylvania

Q: Where can a cat sit that you can't?

A: Your lap.

Q: How many cats can you put in an empty box?

A: Only one because then the box isn't empty.

Q: Why do cats sleep all day?

A: Because they can.

Q: Why can't you ever trust an atom?

A: Because they make up everything.

Q: Why did the book join the police force?

A: Because it wanted to go undercover!

Q: When do you know a tiger isn't telling the truth?

A: When it's a lion.

Q: What does a possum like to do for fun?

A: Hang out with its friends.

Q: How do fleas travel from one cat to another?

A: They itchhike!

Kevin: I'm reading a book about gravity.

Rascal: Is it any good?

Kevin: I can't put it down.

Q: Where did the beaver put its money?

A: In the river bank.

Q: Why did the cat go bowling?

A: It was an alley cat.

Rascal: How does a snowman like his birch beer?

Kevin: In a frosted mug.

Q: What's a dinosaur's favorite snack?

A: Macaroni and trees.

Q: What do you call a dinosaur with an extensive vocabulary?

A: A thesaurus.

Q: What do you call a sleeping prehistoric reptile?

A: A dinosnore.

Q: What do you get when you cross a dinosaur with a kangaroo?

A: A tricera-hops.

Q: What is it called when a cat wins a dog show?

A: A cat-has-trophy.

Q: What's a pirate's favorite fish?

A: A swordfish.

Kevin: Why do bears paint their faces yellow?

Rascal: I don't know. Why?

Kevin: So they can hide in banana trees.

Rascal: Impossible! I've never seen a bear in a banana tree.

Kevin: See? It works!

Q: What's a skunk's favorite sandwich?

A: Peanut butter and smelly.

Q: What did the otter say to the movie star?

A: Can I get your otter-graph?

Q: How do slugs begin fairy tales?

A: "Once upon a slime..."

Q: What do you call an undercover arachnid?

A: A spy-der.

Q: What did the nut say when it sneezed?

A: Cashew!

Q: What do you call a pig that plays basketball?

A: A ball hog.

Q: What do you call a pig that knows karate?

A: A pork chop.

Q: Why do porcupines never lose games?

A: Because they always have the most points.

Q: Why did the cyclops stop teaching?

A: Because he had only one pupil.

Q: What does a ghost put on its bagel?

A: Scream cheese.

Q: What happened when the werewolf swallowed a clock?

A: He got ticks.

Q: What do you get if you cross a dinosaur with a wizard?

A: Tyrannosaurus hex.

Q: What does a panda cook with?

A: A pan, duh.

Knock, knock

Who's there?

Witches.

Witches who?

Witches the way to go home?

Q: Why does a flamingo stand on one leg?

A: Because if it lifted both legs, it would fall over.

Q: What bird can lift the most weight?

A: A crane.

Q: Why did the sea gull fly over the sea?

A: Because if he flew over the bay, he'd be a bagel.

Q: What bird never goes to the barber?

A: A bald eagle.

Q: What did the gorilla call his wife?

A: His prime mate.

Q: What do you call a monkey with all his bananas taken away?

A: Furious George.

Q: Why is Peter Pan always flying?

A: He neverlands (this joke never gets old).

Q: Why did the raccoon cross the road?

A: To prove to the possum that it could be done.

Kevin: What has nine legs, twenty eyes, and purple fur?

Rascal: I don't know.

Kevin: I don't know either, but it's crawling up your leg!

Q: What did the grape say when the raccoon stepped on it?

A: Nothing, it just let out a little wine.

Q: When does a raccoon go "moo"?

A: When he is learning a new language.

A boy lost his favorite book while he was hiking in the Pennsylvania Grand Canyon. Three weeks later, a raccoon walked up to him carrying the book in its mouth. The boy couldn't believe his eyes. He took his favorite book out of the raccoon's mouth, and exclaimed, "It's a miracle!" "Not really," said the raccoon. "Your name is written inside the cover."

A man in a movie theater notices what looks like a raccoon sitting next to him. "Are you a raccoon?" asked the surprised man. "Yes." "What are you doing at the movies?" The raccoon replied, "Well, I liked the book."

Q: What are the clumsiest things in the galaxy?

A: Falling stars.

Q: Why did the moon stop eating?

A: It was full.

Q: What does Saturn like to read?

A: Comet books.

Kevin: Knock, knock

Rascal: Who's there?

Kevin: Ketchup.

Rascal: Ketchup who?

Kevin: Ketchup or else you'll be late for snacks!

Q: Why didn't the nose want to go to school?

A: Because he didn't want picked on.

Q: What's at the bottom of the ocean and shivers?

A: A nervous wreck.

Q: How do you make a tissue dance?

A: Put a little boogie in it.

Q: Why are school cafeteria workers so mean?

A: Because they beat eggs, whip cream, and batter fish.

Q: What vegetables do librarians like?

A: Quiet peas.

Kevin: There are forty fish in a tank. Twenty go on vacation. How many are left?

Rascal: Well, forty minus twenty is...

Kevin: Fish don't go on vacation, silly.

Q: Where did the pencil go on vacation?

A: Pennsylvania.

Q: Why did the elephant get upset on vacation?

A: He forgot to pack his trunk.

Q: Where do books sleep?

A: Under their covers.

Q: When is a door not a door?

A: When it's ajar.

Q: What gets wetter the more it dries?

A: A towel.

Q: What has teeth but can't eat?

A: A comb.

Q: What do you call a raccoon with a carrot in each ear?

A: Anything you want. He can't hear you.

Q: How does a polar bear build its house?

A: Igloos it together.

Q: What does a rain cloud wear under its clothes?

A: Thunderwear.

Q: What did summer say to spring?

A: "Help! I'm going to fall."

Q: Why does lightning shock people?

A: Because it doesn't know how to conduct itself.

Q: If April showers bring May flowers, what do May flowers bring?

A: Pilgrims.

Kevin: Did you hear about the cat whose left paw fell off?

Rascal: No, how is she doing?

Kevin: She's all right now!

Kevin: Have you heard the the joke about the germ?

Rascal: No, tell me.

Kevin: Never mind... I don't want it to spread.

Rascal: Why are your jokes so painfully funny?

Kevin: Must be the punch line.

Q: What is the best kind of book to read when you have a cold?

A: Sinus fiction.

Q: How do rodents freshen their breath?

A: With mousewash.

Q: What do you get when you throw books into the ocean?

A: A title wave.

Q: Why can't your nose be 12 inches long?

A: Because then it would be a foot.

Q: What is the world's tallest building?

A: The library, because it has the most stories.

Q: What can go through water and not get wet?

A: Sunlight.

Q: What kind of phone does a turtle use?

A: A shell phone.

Q: What do you call someone with no body and no nose?

A: Nobody knows.

Do you want to hear a joke about paper?
Never mind, it's tearable.

Q: Why did Gyspy the Cat throw the clock out the window?

A: Because she heard time flies.

Q: What is red and moves up and down?

A: A tomato in an elevator.

Q: What type of car does a raccoon drive?

A: A Furrari.

Q: What do you call a boomerang that doesn't come back?

A: A stick.

Kevin: I'd like a new boomerang, but I can't seem to throw the old one away.

Q: How do you communicate with the Loch Ness Monster?

A: Drop her a line.

Q: What followed the dinosaur?

A: Its tail.

Q: When do zombies play tricks on each other?

A: On April Ghoul's Day.

Q: What's a ghost's favorite fruit?

A: A Boonana!

Q: What kind of monster is safe to put in the washing machine?

A: A wash and wear wolf.

Q: Why did the haunted house dislike storms?

A: Because the rain dampened its spirits.

Q: Where do baby ghosts go during the day?

A: Day scare centers.

Q: What type of street does a ghost like best?

A: A dead end.

Q: What do you get when dinosaurs crash their cars?

A: Tyrannosaurus wrecks!

Q: What would you get if you crossed a dinosaur with a pig?

A: Jurassic pork!

Q: What is a monster's favorite drink?

A: Demonade.

Q: What type of book did the zombie like to read?

A: One with a cemetery plot.

Q: Why are fish so smart?

A: They are always in schools.

Q: What's the best day to eat bacon?

A: Fryday.

Q: How do you fix a broken pumpkin?

A: With a pumpkin patch.

Q: How does a bird with a broken wing manage to land safely?

A: With a sparrowchute!

Q: What do you call a cat with eight legs that likes to swim?

A: An octopuss!

Did you see the horse that could balance a corncob on its head? It was some unique corn.

Q: Why did the dog jump into the water?

A: He wanted to chase the catfish.

Q: What's a cat's favorite TV show?

A: The evening mews.

Q: What kind of fish will help you hear better?

A: A herring aid!

Q: What cat purrs more than any other?

A: A Purrsian.

Q: Why was the cat afraid of the tree?

A: It was afraid of its bark.

Q: What runs all day but never gets tired?

A: A river.

Q: What is the smelliest job in the army?

A: Driving a septic tank.

Q: How did the superhero get a pain in the ribs?

A: He got a sidekick.

Show me a forgetful superhero and I'll show you a crime fighter who can't remember his secret identity.

Q: What does a superhero use to keep his mask in place?

A: Masking tape.

Q: Why are there no good zombie comedians?

A: Because zombies are always dead serious.

Q: What do you get when you cross a baseball player and an alien* space craft?

A: A pitcher and a saucer.

*For more about aliens, check out *The Totally Ninja Raccoons Meet the Little Green Men*.

Q: What baseball position does the Abominable Snowman play?

A: Frost base.

Q: What's the best way to hit an Italian meatball?

A: Use a mozzarella stick.

Q: What kind of Mexican food do you find on a beach?

A: Taco shells.

Q: What does a beaver's diet consist of?

A: Tree square meals a day.

Q: What illness can you catch from a ninja?

A: Kung flu.

Q: What do you put at the end of a cafeteria sentence?

A: A lunch period.

Q: What did the math teacher do when she had too many students?

A: She divided the class.

Kevin: Knock, knock

Rascal: Who's there?

Kevin: It's Tory.

Rascal: It's Tory who?

Kevin: It's Tory time. Read me a book.

Kevin: I went to baseball school to learn how to steal bases.

Rascal: How did you do?

Kevin: I got thrown out.

Q: What is the favorite name for werewolves?

A: Harry!

Q: Why don't wizards like to cast spells on boats?

A: They get potion sickness.

Q: What do witches use to open haunted houses?

A: A spooo-key!

Q: Where do witches go when they run out of eye of newt?

A: The gross-ery store!

Q: What did Bigfoot plant in his garden?

A: Sa-squash!

Q: What do you call a messy creature in a lake?

A: The Loch Mess monster!

Q: Why do dragons sleep all day?

A: So they can get out at knights.

Q: What do you call bird ghosts?

A: Sea-ghouls!

Q: What did the witch call the birds that haunted her backyard?

A: Polter-geese.

Q: What do you call a tent for a zombie?

A: A cree-pee!

Q: What type of dogs do zombies own?

A: Rot-weilers!

Q: What did the king call the stone felines guarding his castle?

A: Cat-er-pillars!

Q: What do you feed an Italian ghost?

A: Spook-ghetti!

Q: What do you call a zombie's hair?

A: Mouldy locks!

Q: What do you get when you cross a hyena and a banana?

A: Peels of laughter!

Q: Where do zombies go swimming?

A: In the Dead Sea!

Q: What do you get when you cross a cow and a washing machine?

A: A milk shake!

Q: When did the dragon get full?

A: About mid-knight!

Q: Why was the tree feeling low?

A: It was stumped!

Q: What goes up but never comes down?

A: Your age.

Q: What do you always get on your birthday?

A: Another year older.

Q: Where do pigs park their cars?

A: The pork-ing lot!

Q: What do sea monsters eat for dinner?

A: Fish and ships.

Q: What do you get when you cross a pig and a tree?

A: A porky-pine!

Q: What's as big as an elephant but weighs nothing?

A: Its shadow!

Q: What did the alien say to the garden?

A: Take me to your weeder!

Q: How do you make an octopus laugh?

A: With ten-tickles!

Q: Why does a dog wag its tail?

A: Because no one will wag it for him!

Q: How does an ocean say hello?

A: It waves!

Q: What room can you not go in?

A: A mushroom!

Q: What disappears when you stand up?

A: Your lap!

Q: What did Gypsy the Cat say when she sat on her rubber duckie?

A: I've got a crush on you!

Q: What does a slice of toast wear to bed?

A: Jam-mies!

Q: What runs around all day and lies under the bed with its tongue hanging out?

A: A sneaker.

Q: Why did the belt get arrested?

A: It held up a pair of pants.

Q: How do you make bears listen to bedtime stories?

A: Take away the B, and they're all ears.

Q: What is a cat's favorite bedtime story?

A: *Three Blind Mice.*

Q: How do you know if there's a dinosaur under your bed?

A: Your nose touches the ceiling.

Q: How do you know if a dinosaur is in your shower?

A: You can't close the curtain.

Q: What does Bigfoot climb to get to his bedroom?

A: Mon-stairs.

Q: Why did the werewolf take a bite out of the tightrope walker?

A: He wanted to have a well-balanced diet.

Q: What did the monkey say when his tail got caught in a fan?

A: "It won't be long now."

Q: How do pigs communicate?

A: In swine language.

Q: What do beavers eat for breakfast?

A: Oakmeal.

Q: What animal needs to wear a wig?

A: A bald eagle.

Q: What do you get when you cross a turtle and a porcupine?

A: A slow poke.

Q: What do you call a rude cow?

A: Beef jerky.

Q: What do you get when you cross a pig with a centipede?

A: Bacon and legs.

Q: What do you call a bear with no teeth?

A: A gummy bear.

Q: Where do cows get their medicine?

A: The farmacy.

Q: Did you hear the joke about the skunk?

A: Never mind, it really stinks.

Q: What did the Sphinx Cat say when she got a comb for her birthday?

A: "Thanks, I'll never part with it."

Q: Why did dinosaurs eat raw meat?

A: Because they didn't know how to cook.

Q: What do polar bears like to eat?

A: Ice-berg-ers.

Q: What do you call a werewolf with a fever?

A: A hot dog.

Q: What do you call a werewolf that uses bad language?

A: A swearwolf.

Q: How do you make a werewolf laugh?

A: Give it a funny bone.

Q: How does a werewolf eat ice cream?

A: With its mouth, like anyone else.

Q: What was the werewolf in the butcher shop arrested for?

A: Chop-lifting.

Q: What do you call a cold werewolf?

A: A chilli dog.

Q: What do you get when you cross a werewolf and a hyena?

A: A monster with a sense of humor.

Q: How does a werewolf eat an elephant?

A: One bite at a time.

Q: What did the werewolf eat after getting his teeth cleaned?

A: The dentist.

Q: Where do vampires keep their money?

A: In the blood bank.

Q: Why do vampires need cold medicine?

A: For their coffin.

Q: Why do vampires chew gum?

A: Because they have bat breath.

Two zebras are at a watering hole.

One says to the other, "Hey what did you have for lunch?"

The other says, "Serengeti and meatballs."

Q: What's the best time of day to schedule a dentist appointment?

A: Tooth Hurty

Q: Where do polar bears vote?

A: The North Poll!

Q: What do you call people who are afraid of Santa Claus?

A: Claustrophobic.

Kevin: Knock, knock

Rascal: Who's there?

Kevin: Murray.

Rascal: Murray who?

Kevin: Murray Christmas!

Q: What happens when a banana gets sunburnt?

A: It starts to peel.

Q: What birds spend all their time on their knees?

A: Birds of prey!

Kevin: Why should you wait an hour after eating before you go swimming?

Bandit: Actually, there's no need to wait an hour. I just use caution.

Kevin: Because you'll get a Krampus*

Bandit: That simply just isn't true.

Kevin: Why does Krampus always go down the chimney?

A: Because it soots him.

*For more about Krampus, check out *The Totally Ninja Raccoons and the Catmas Caper.*

Q: What is twenty feet tall, has sharp teeth and goes Ho Ho Ho?

A: Tyranno-santa Rex!

Q: What does Santa use when he goes fishing?

A: His north pole!

Q: Who delivers Christmas presents to pets?

A: Why Santa Paws of course!

About the Author

Kevin Coolidge is currently the author of eleven children's books and the creator of the Totally Ninja Raccoons. He's available for school presentations from kindergarten to 4th grade. Presentations include providing information on the writing process and encouraging fun in literacy.

He's especially good with kids, but is open to speaking with other groups as well. As a bookstore owner, Kevin can talk about books, small business, literacy, and most aspects of popular culture, in addition to his books. He resides in Wellsboro, PA, just a short hike from the Pennsylvania Grand Canyon.

When he's not writing, you can find him at *From My Shelf Books & Gifts*, an independent bookstore he runs with his lovely wife, Kasey; several helpful employees; and two friendly bookstore cats, Huck & Finn.

He's recently become an honorary member of the Cat Board, and when he's not scooping the litter boxes, getting status reports on the squirrels, or feeding Gypsy her tuna, he's writing more stories about the Totally Ninja Raccoons.

Kevin children's series, *The Totally Ninja Raccoons*, is specifically geared to reluctant readers. Be sure to catch their next big adventure, *The Totally Ninja Raccoons Discover the Lost World*.

You can write him at:

From My Shelf Books & Gifts
7 East Ave., Suite 101
Wellsboro, PA 16901

www.wellsborobookstore.com

About the Illustrator

Jubal Lee is a former Wellsboro resident who now resides in sunny Florida, due to his extreme allergic reaction to cold weather.

He is an eclectic artist who, when not drawing raccoons, thunderbirds, and the like, enjoys writing, bicycling, and short walks on the beach.

Get your own copies of the adventures with the Totally Ninja Raccoons!

The Totally Ninja Raccoons Meet Bigfoot

_____ copies @ $5.99 each = _____

The Totally Ninja Raccoons Meet the Weird & Wacky Werewolf

_____ copies @ $5.99 each = _____

The Totally Ninja Raccoons and the Secret of the Canyon

_____ copies @ $5.99 each = _____

The Totally Ninja Raccoons Meet the Thunderbird

_____ copies @ $5.99 each = _____

The Totally Ninja Raccoons and the Catmas Caper

_____ copies @ $6.99 each = _____

The Totally Ninja Raccoons and the Secret of Nessmuk Lake

_____ copies @ $6.99 each = _____

The Totally Ninja Raccoons Meet the Little Green Men

_____ copies @ $6.99 each = _____

The Totally Ninja Raccoons Meet the Jersey Devil

_____ copies @ $6.99 each = _____

Subtotal = _____

$2.99 shipping = _____
(15 books or less)

Total Enclosed = _____

Send this form, with payment via check or money order, to:

From My Shelf Books & Gifts
7 East Ave., Suite 101
Wellsboro, PA 16901

or call **(570) 724-5793**
Also available at **wellsborobookstore.com**